THE BOOK
About
Branka

ŽELJKO VUJOVIĆ

ZELJKO VUJOVIC

THE BOOK ABOUT BRANKA

EXCERPTS FROM THE BOOK
IN THE CHAOTIC MURMUR OF AN UNCLEAR DESTINY

ARPress
ILLUMINATING IDEAS,
EMPOWERING VOICES

ARPress
45 Dan Road Suite 5
Canton, MA 02021

Hotline: 1(888) 821-0229
Fax: 1(508) 545-7580

Ordering Information:
Quantity sales. Special discounts are available on quantity purchases by corporations, associations, and others. For details, contact the publisher at the address above.

Printed in the United States of America.

ISBN-13:   Softcover   979-8-89330-677-4
              eBook   979-8-89330-676-7

Library of Congress Control Number: 2024902467

TABLE OF CONTENTS

Branka was born in Trebinje on June 3, 1953, to father Radonja Đukić and mother Ilinka Đukić, née Zeković.

The Đukići, the ancestors on the father's side, were originally from the Pješivci tribe. They settled in Studence near Nikšić, after the Berlin Congress in 1878, when that area belonged to Montenegro. The Zekovići, the ancestors on the mother's side, came from the area around the villages of Tušina and Mljetičak, in Drobnjak. They moved and lived in Nikšić.

She moved to Titograd (Podgorica) in 1958 with her father, mother, and brother. Her father died in 1967 when she was 14 years old. She graduated from the "Savo Pejanović" Elementary School, the "Slobodan Škerović" Gymnasium, and the Faculty of Law in Titograd (Podgorica) in the regular term.

Immediately after graduating from law school, she got a job at "Zetatraans". She spent her working life in "Zetatrans" until her retirement on 12/30/2011.

BIRDHOUSE

Already on the seventh day, it rained
as if with me the whole world
was forgotten
but you smiled
and the sky smiled
at the same moment

And you flipped through your life
and the stars sparkled into my life
and then you kissed me
like a bird knocking
on your window

**I am celebrating the day of your love tonight
in the birdhouse, in the house for two**

And while I'm telling you about us,
you look at me and smile
because you know it all

Even though the days pass,
the birds still come
to our window

**I am celebrating the day of your love tonight
in the birdhouse, in the house for two**

Gabi Novak sings

Authors: Drago Britvić and Arsen Dedić,
Source: https://www.youtube.com/watch?v=0I2ckIXc7Zs
Licenses: [Merlin] Croatia Records (on behalf of Croatia Records), and 2 Music
Rights Societies, Podgorica, 18.12.2

1

I APPROACH THE WINDOW THROUGH THE CITY WALKING AUTUMN

Forty years have passed in this condition on the sixth floor. It's autumn again. I moved, for the umpteenth time, the curtain at the right end of the window. In front of me, below, is the building of the Kindergarten "Đina Vrbica". The yard is fenced. Grass park with furniture. Slide, sand pool, metal bed with bars for children. They grasp the crossbar with their fists, higher above the ground, and move from one crossbar to another with the strength of their arm muscles. My three children finished attending this kindergarten a long time ago. I'm looking at him. It's hard for me to turn back and look around the apartment. I see her! I am aware of every detail of the apartment even when I am not in it. Living room. In the middle is a small, square, glass table, covered in disorder with several books and a notebook in which I write various notes, bills for used electricity, water, garbage collection, and apartment tax. In the corner of the room, a TV that I stopped turning on. I am fed up with what I have seen all these years, during which he did not move from that place, from that angle. Two couches against two opposite walls, two armchairs in which he can gently rock when he sits in them. On the wall, opposite the window, is a shelf with books and framed photos. Three drawers for documents, four cabinets, two at the top, and two at the bottom. In the lockers are binders with documents, diplomas, and certificates. Most of the documents have expired. They exist without meaning. There are also albums with pictures of events from life, which has passed, mostly, in these last forty years, my life and the lives of those who lived in this state. To the left is the dining room with a large round table, which has not been used for a long time for its basic purpose. On the right, by the wall, is the piano, on which the daughter practiced playing when she was a high school student.

To the left of the dining room, is a classic kitchen, separated from the dining room by a wall in the form of a bar. There is an electric stove, a refrigerator, a kitchen display case with a worktop, and more police on the walls, in which there are many dishes. I don't know how I would use it. My wife got it and sometimes used it when she prepared festive lunches for our grown children. The kitchen leads to a glazed balcony, which I also stopped going out to. Sometimes, very rarely, it happens to me that I take a step or two for a short time. In the second part of the apartment, there are two rooms, a small hallway, and a bathroom in the middle. The room, on the south side, towards Lake Skadar and the sea, has access to a small balcony, on which there are lines for drying clothes. I sleep in another room, on the north side, towards the hill of Gorica. It now has only one bed, two chests of drawers, and two bookshelves on the opposite walls of the room. The three-door wardrobe is in the right corner when you enter the room, leaning against two walls. It has a lot more wardrobe than I use. I don't know what to do with so many wardrobes. My movement in the state is mostly limited to lying on the couch in the living room, opening the fridge, eating at the bar counter, washing the dishes superficially, and going to bed for a night's sleep. It invigorates me when I happen to take an hour's nap, in the afternoon, in that bed. In the front of the apartment is a small hallway with a shelf for shoes on one wall, and across the street is a pantry with shelves on the wall, filled with objects, which I don't think I ever use. The utility room is dominated by a washing machine. I remember being here I bought it a long time ago and participated in its installation, but I have never used it personally. My wife used it. Now I will teach you to use it. So far, this storage room has been the most useful for storing my backpack with hiking equipment, hiking boots, and hiking poles. I'm tired of thinking that I should arrange, and clean the whole apartment and all the rugs in it. (10/19/2022)

◊

When you see everything, analyze, understand, and decide, you return to your apartment, where you are bound by memories and all emotions live in it. You have to live, look forward to each day that comes, and of course, remember the past. A man must not be alone but surrounded by people, children, grandchildren, and society, with the definition of life: "Everything that comes, I am next to it"!

◊

Forty years have passed in this apartment on the sixth floor. It's autumn again...

THE CHILD IS THE FATHER OF A MAN

Picture 1. With Grandma (Gift of Stnka Zeković-Poleksić)

Picture 2. With cow (Gift of Stnka Zeković-Poleksić)

Did this little girl remain herself? Why does she need a watch on her wrist? Is she happy, without any reason, just by being there, next to the grandmother and next to the cow, on the outskirts of Nikšić? What does he offer to the grandmother, with an outstretched hand, in a small bowl? She is so big that she can freely stand next to the cow, hold the rope tied around the cow's horns with her left hand, and grab the cow by the neck with her right.

STUDENT AGE

Picture 3. On the Boulevard in front of the Post Office

Who is this beautiful, smiling, forgotten girl in high-heeled shoes, jeans, a plaid shirt, with glasses? Who are these guys? Why is everyone looking at her and everything revolves around her?

SUMMER OF 1977

Corso in Freedom Street. Summer vacation after the end of the last, tenth semester (graduate internship) at the Faculty of Electrical Engineering in Belgrade. I go out several nights in a row. I stand on the sidewalk across from the "Department Store" and observe. I'm looking. I am looking for a girl who will like me. I choose. Walkers pass from one end of the street to the other and back. I spotted a group of three girls. They walked together every evening. One of them, on the side, was my friend from school, my generation, but I liked the girl in the middle. She was nicely sunbathed, with a tanned face. Blue blouse, white skirt, sandals. The most beautiful girl on the Corso that summer. I started watching her, openly, every night. The girls noticed this and said to each other: "Željko is looking at you." I called my school friend and asked her to introduce me to the friend she was walking with. She met us. We shook hands and went for ice cream on the terrace of Hotel "Crna Gora". I told her that I was studying. I told her that I had passed all the exams and that I was preparing my thesis. She told me that she has already graduated and is working.

She paid for the ice cream. She didn't want to hear or allow another possibility.

The summer passed and the month of January came very quickly. I looked for her and told her that I graduated. We went to the Green Lounge of Hotel "Crna Gora" to celebrate.

That's how it started.

MEASUREMENT TIME

Picture 4. On Duklja

Spring has arrived, so to speak, immediately. We scheduled meetings at the fountain in Ulica slobode. It is the only fountain on Freedom Street. In the upper part of the Street, across from the famous pastry shop Š.T. Hamza.

I usually wore light clothing, sports pants, a shirt, and a white sweater. Footwear, shoes that I liked. Wide, comfortable yellow moccasins. Because of them, she called me "Yellow Duck".

We went on day trips to the sea by car. Around the city and its surroundings, on foot. One of those trips is the one in the picture, taken at the archaeological excavations in Duklja.

Did we measure up? Bearing in mind that, like this, she put her hand over my shoulder, and stood taller than me, it could be taken as a sure indication that we were measuring each other.

PREVIOUS TO THE WEDDING

Sometimes we used to take a taxi around the city. We were sitting in the back seat. On one occasion, our hands were on the seat, and they came close and touched. I felt it, and she also told me that she shivered from that touch.

I asked her, in the taxi: were you married, although I was sure of an affirmative answer.

She remained silent and confirmed that she would.

Preparations for the wedding have begun. She, with her friends, was choosing a wedding dress. She ordered a wedding dress from Ričard Gumzej from Zagreb. He was the most famous designer of wedding dresses in Yugoslavia. I was planning to be the groom in a white suit with a dark tie. And so it would.

Picture 5. The bride signs her name in the Marriage Book

HONEYMOON

We spent our honeymoon in August 1980 on Hvar for a week, at the "Solaris" auto camp near Šibenik, and in Bled, Slovenia, for a week.

We left Tiotgarad by bus and arrived in Drvenik, a town in southern Dalmatia, between Makarska and Ploče. The blue sky was dotted with reddish-ruddy clouds, which retained the reflections of the last rays of the setting sun. We managed to run into the last ferry, which, that day, was transporting passengers to Sućuraj on Hvar.

We slept in Sućuraj, and the next day, by bus, on a narrow, winding road, in the middle of the island, through the karst, the waterless area with water cisterns in the fields, in some places, we headed to the town of Hvar. On the higher, steep elevations, there were thickets, very dense groups of low trees, and tall bushes. On the lower slopes, thickets change to pine forests. We passed by Jelsa and Stari Grad and, after several hours of driving, arrived in Hvar. Desired, targeted, and challenging destination. Accommodation in a private house awaited us, previously secured through a tourist organization. The house was located high on the hill, with a view of the Hvar port, the town, and the surrounding area. A neat room with a double bed, fluffy, sparkling clean white sheets, and the smell of lavender in the room. In front of the house, the front part of the house, an open terrace with tables for serving meals. Fish and wine. Enjoyment. Food to enjoy. Fish, fish, and wine. Morning, early, departure to port. We buy two kilos of peaches, picked in the Neretva Valley, and brought them here for tourists to enjoy eating their juices.

The Aboat driver took us by boat to the island of Stipanska. On the other side of the island, along a small bay, all naturally covered with stepped stone slabs. All day sunbathing and swimming in clear, transparent sea water. Complete physical and mental rest. Paradise. Another world. In the evening, the boatman took us back to the port. From there to the host, dinner. Fish and wine. It was like that for three or four days. After that, the boatman suggested that we go swimming on the island of Jerolimo, a little closer to Hvar, right next to Stipanska island. We accepted. Beautiful beach, lots of bathers, view of the city and port, lots of sun and sea. Beauty and wonder. Seven days passed in a flash, but they remained unforgettable.

From the port of Hvar, we went by boat to Šibenik. Entering the beautiful bay of Šibenik was an event and experience of a special kind. My sister and brother-in-law were waiting for us. We spent the first night at their house. We were at the "Solaris" auto camp all day. During the day, sunbathe and swim on the beaches of "Solaris" and walks through the surrounding cypress park. Seven days. Seven days of sea, sun, lounging, and walking in the shade of cypress trees. Rest and recovery continue.

On the eighth day, in the evening, we got on the bus and headed along the Croatian coast to Slovenia, to Bled. In Bled, accommodation in a private house, with a woman whose husband had died not long before. Now she is engaged in tourism. Rural (peasant) tourism.

Lake Bled with Bled Castle is located on the only natural island in Slovenia. We rented a boat to ride on the lake, row to the castle, and see the castle. We walked around the lake. They rode their bikes through the beautiful villages around the lake.

A lot of greenery. Trees strewn with white flowers. I recorded everything with a camera, to keep a memory of those wonderful days.

We set aside one day to visit Lake Bohinj, which is about thirty minutes away from Lake Bled. We went to the Savica waterfall, a double waterfall in the shape of the letter A. The water bursts out in the middle of the cliff wall and falls 78 meters into a wonderful, green pool. From there it continues along the stream of the same name, which, as the main source, flows into Lake Bohinj, and flows from Lake Bohinj as the source of the river Sava Bohinjka. After the Savica waterfall, that day we went up by cable car (gondola) for four minutes, from the shore of the lake to the ski station Vogel. From there, by cable car, to the last station, Eagle's head. From there, on foot, approximately one hour, to the mountain top of Sija. It was cold on that hill. We did not expect a such cold and we were not prepared for it. Us in a light summer wardrobe. I gave Branka my sweater to ease her chattering teeth from November. We successfully returned, by cable car.

The seventh, and last day of our stay in Bled is approaching. I carefully calculate how much money we have spent and make sure that we have enough left over so that we don't have enough to return home.

We went to Zagreb from Bled, and from Zagreb, by plane, to Titograd. My mother and father were waiting for us at the airport.

The next day I rushed to the photographer to develop the film from the camera and take pictures, which I took all the time, from Drvenik, through Hvar, Solaris, Bled, Bohinj, Savica, Vogel... The photographer opened the camera lid and showed me. There was no film in the camera. I was surprised, stunned, and disappointed. The whole time I was taking pictures and clicking with an empty camera. So, from this honeymoon, not a single photo remained, for a memory, except this memory of mine.

OWN FAMILY HOUSEHOLD

We rented an apartment in Vukice Mitrović Street, under Gorica, and started running a joint household. We bought food together, but she cooked and prepared the food. Before noon, we each went to our work, our place of work.

It was autumn. Two months have passed since the wedding. She started to welcome me and aggressively aim at me.

Why am I not pregnant? My brother's wife immediately remained in a different state.

I was confused, taken aback, and surprised. Am I, not the one who is in charge, who takes care of the pregnancy, and for whom the offspring is created? I did not expect something like this from my wife.

The tension soon subsided because, the following month, she received a report from the doctor that she was pregnant. For her, the doctor's report, and for me, pride and satisfaction.

◊

Summer came quickly. Grandpa Mijajlo came to Stara Varoš. He stopped in front of the house, took out a gun from his belt, and fired three shots, high into the air, towards the sky. Let it burst, let it resound, let it be heard up to the sky! A male child was born! First, a man!

A PRINCESS WITH HER FIRST BABY

Picture 6. With her firstborn son

NEW BEAUTIFUL BRENNA

We moved into the apartment in March 1983. It took three more months for the firstborn son to turn two years old, and a month and a half for the still-unborn daughter to be born. Branka's stomach had grown in the eighth month. She occasionally complained of lower back pain. I helped her lie down on the couch and massaged her back with my hands and an electric massager that we had bought. The pain did not stop. Somewhere, in the first days of May, I had the idea that it would be good to warm her back. This is how they work in physical therapy when they treat those with back pain. She lay down on the couch. I put a thick blanket on her back and passed over it with a heated iron to transfer heat to her. I don't remember if it was on the first or second day when she started screaming in pain. We rushed her to the hospital and she gave birth. The baby was born with thick, black hair, and the doctor on duty exclaimed: Here she is! New Beautiful Brena was born! So I, ironing Branka's back with a hot iron over the blanket, hastened to prevent her from staying too long in her mother's stomach, but to give birth to a daughter, New Beautiful Brena.

TIME OF ANNUAL HOLIDAYS ON THE CROATIAN COAST

Summer 1982, hidden Luka on Lastovo, and in 1984 Postire on Brač, Komiža on Vis, one day on Biševo and Solaris near Šibenik.

Picture 7. With daughter and son at Krka Falls

We were on the island of Brač from 03.08.1985. to 17.08.1985. year, first in Milna (7 days), and then in Postira (7 days). We swam in Osibova Bay. We visited Supetar, Bol, and Splitska, and passed through Sumartin. We climbed Vidova Gora (778 m above sea level), the highest mountain peak of all the islands in the Adriatic Sea.

Bojana, Srđan, Branka i Željko

Postira, 15.08.1985. years

Picture 8. Summer vacation in 1985.

Summer 1987 on Jaz near Budva, and 1988 on Velika plaža near Ulcinj. I am satisfied. A happy father with his wife and children.

Picture 9. With Zvjezdan on Big beach, Ulcinj

LAWYER IN WORK ORGANIZATION

In parallel with her family life, Branka very conscientiously worked as a lawyer in a labor organization. It impressed me. I loved having a wife like that. In this picture, you can see the attentive expression on the face of a young, tidy employee with short hair, who calmly and purposefully follows and participates in the work conversation.

Picture 10. Lawyer in the Legal Service and Secretary of the Labor Organization

Employees in the work organization appreciated and respected her because of her work characteristics and the human relationship with employees. I am looking at this photo from a fun-friendly evening, organized by the Labor Organization. I look at this smile, this face, these eyes, this long, white, folded scarf, draped over both shoulders, this dark dress... I loved Branka like that.

21

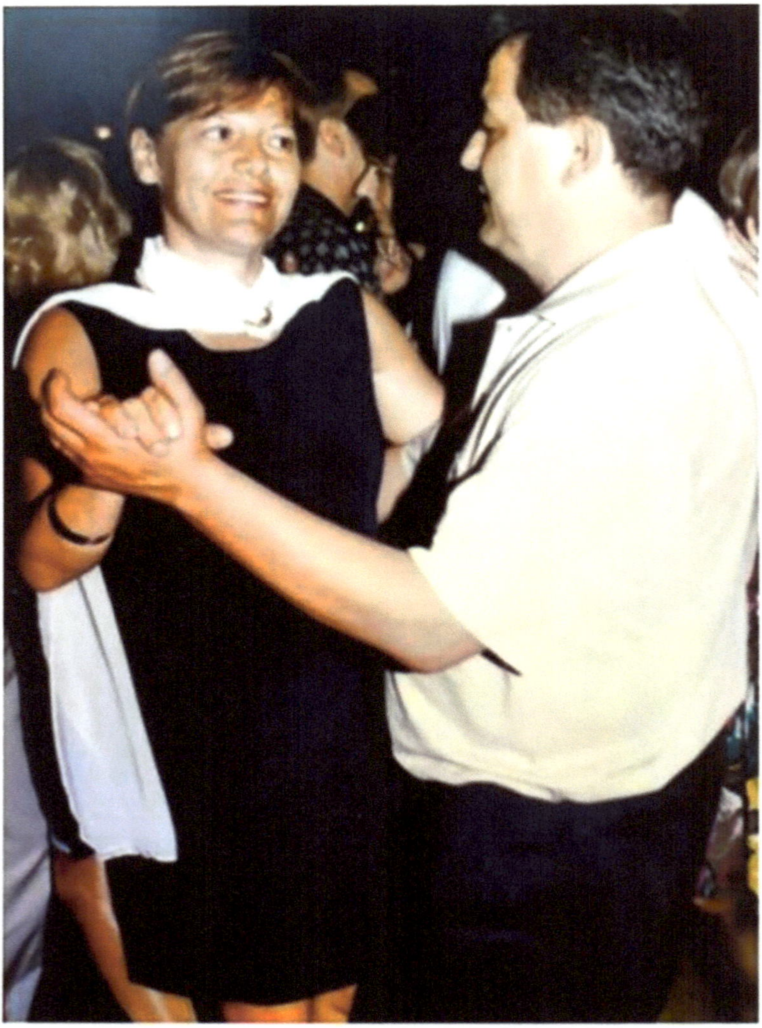

![Picture 11]

Picture 11. A fun evening of the Working Organization

ONE LETTER DATED OCTOBER 12, 1991

Taking upon ourselves the obligation to write a professional, objective, and as useful letter as possible for you, we found ourselves faced with a certain dilemma whether to comment only on the facts presented in your letter, or to try to find out some items that you did not mention, but did not - as they imply. We have decided to stay on the platform of facts, which we hope you will use objectively, usefully, and above all adequately to get out of your current problems.

There is no doubt that the problems of the family, in general, will become more and more prominent because this is imposed by the social, political, and economic climate. Of course, it is impossible to speak in general, in the form of a solid and strictly defined scheme. But it is obvious that you also formed a more or less transformed, but still patriarchal family with established family relationships. However, we should not lose sight of the fact that family relationships change - as the years of marriage go by, as children grow up and impose their own rules of the game. Problems, discomforts, and difficulties arise because people and their understandings change much more slowly than the newly formed family structure. An important item is also a stable economic situation, which, in your case, seems to be satisfactory. We emphasize this because, you will agree with us, changes in the material and economic basis of the family are often a condition for changing the entire family structure and its relationships.

In the personal life of an individual, it is normal that the importance of the family is great. However, increasing the family causes qualitatively different relations among its members. The positive thing is that each individual in the extended family is increasingly enriched as a person. But, with the increase in the number of members, the obligations of all members also increase. Very often, spouses who, at the beginning of their marriage, were completely devoted to each other, drift apart. On the other hand, strong bonds are created between the woman (mother) and the children.

You are satisfied that your wife is a good mother, but you found yourself in a situation for which you were not sufficiently prepared - that your wife is moving away from you. The stage of neglecting your spouse (in this case - you) hides the danger that the spouses will become too far apart, that there will be emotional coldness, intolerance, infidelity, and, in the worst case, the disintegration of the family. Since the relationship between you and her changes significantly, your connection weakens, and the common thread is lost. Our time brought the emancipation of women and gave women new rights, but also increased obligations. You start from a bad position if you look for the culprit in you or her. No one is to blame for such events. Such changes occur when something major happens, when one of the parties simply "bursts" from dissatisfaction, or if, on the contrary, nothing happens for a long time, and the monotony of everyday life simply causes such reactions in you and others. To your wife.

Looking from her point of view, things probably look like this - she is burdened with daily obligations at work, at home, and towards her children, and is dissatisfied that the environment (first of all - you, because you are the most important to her) does not notice the extent of her abuses. and her effort, and that all makes room for a feeling of loneliness. Grumbling, nervousness, sigh... it's her alarm, a cry for help. Or, even better, through humming, he wants to tell you: "I need protection, comfort, love, attention!" Notice me, understand me, love me - that's what's most important to me!" You seem to lack the power of perception. As the day goes on, you do not respond to her demands, and normally the result is her punishment with sexual abstinence. You don't understand it and - the circle closes. You two are in the war of the deaf. So where is the exit? The message, it seems to us, is clear - don't walk away! Try to organize an evening just for the two of you once in a while. Take a walk along the old paths, sit in the restaurant where you started to cultivate your love or sit at home reminiscing about old experiences that meant a lot to you... And try to be as gentle as possible. Hand in hand - and all problems will, over time, disappear. This kind of behavior will bring happiness to you and your wife, and of course to your children too - there will be no yelling and arguing and family relations will become more harmonious. Responsibility for your behavior is mutual, but - start first. When someone is almost 40 years old, with a higher education, then he is certainly aware that maturity and responsibility should be the basic model of behavior. Give your wife small, small pleasures during the day. Believe me, women need a little. Use small "men's tricks". Remember how it was easy for you when you were busy and promised eternal and only love? Leave all obligations for a moment and calmly, together, drink coffee, and talk. Sometimes compliment her on her new hairstyle, and shoes, or give her some other compliment. She is crying out for attention. She is probably tired of washing, ironing, and cooking, all in the background, without praise. Is love an art? If it is, it requires knowledge and effort, not something that is born with magic and that overwhelms a person if he is lucky. Your wife, and you too, fall into such a state that can be described as "hunger for love". Remember - women always try to be attractive, groom themselves, and take care of themselves ... Therefore, start to win back your wife and start pleasant conversations, showing goodwill to understand her.

Many times you are not aware of how problems accumulate, so you find yourself in a situation where the circle is closed. Then the struggle begins - how to get out of the vicious circle. The consequence of such a condition is headaches, which are certainly psychosomatic. As the ball unravels, and you and your wife regain intimate emotional contact, sedatives, and big headaches should be a thing of the past. Man's desire for connection in an emotional, and certainly also sexual, sense is the most powerful desire. The inability to satisfy it often leads to illness (ulcers, headaches...). You live together, you need each other, so enrich your own life and stop punishing each other. Enjoy yourself, your family, and all that you have achieved. If you don't take action, you will make yourself feel helpless. Giving must be mutual. The only condition to achieve that harmony between two people is complete emotional closeness. At the same time, for you, as a man, the proof of that closeness is sexual intercourse, and for your wife, as a woman, the proof is a nice word, physical closeness, praise for her appearance, and the effort put in, and sexual intercourse for her come later - as a result of the satisfaction of all of those factors, but also the peak of satisfaction.

Giving is never and can never be deprivation, sacrifice, or abandonment of another. Giving is an experience of one's strength and enrichment. It would be painful and futile to live together and not give. Everyday experience tells us that what a person considers necessary depends a lot on his character. You are there to determine, knowing your wife, what she needs, and when. When you are both in the mood for an open conversation, without outsmarting, or what's worse, physical competition, talk openly about your own intimate life, your hopes, and anxieties. Even showing your anger, hatred or impatience is much better than separation, silence... Mixed, ambivalent feelings are common among married partners and this is tolerated as long as there is a tendency to grow into positive feelings. You will agree that one cannot be intimate only in bed. Sexual desires must be connected with the emotion of love. Your wife wants the desire for the physical union to be combined with your attention and love for her. Otherwise, after the relationship, she will feel like a "thing", used, and misunderstood, and each time she will move further away from you. Tenderness is an integral part of love - both in physical and non-physical forms of love. Loving someone is not only a strong feeling - it is also a decision and a promise. Taking everything into account, we can conclude that you have many chances that can be used to make success complete and final.

The team at the psychological counseling center sends you and your family lots of success, happiness, and mutual understanding.

◊

The psychologist's advice was useful. Happiness returns to the family nest. The children are growing up, and Elijah is getting older.

GUESTS AT A WEDDING IN BELGRADE

Picture 12. Arrival at the wedding, Belgrade, 2005.

Wide smiles, joy in the chest, and pride overwhelmed the mother and son as they solemnly walk, approaching a new celebration, at which the new bride will receive a ceremonial wedding ring on an open stage in Košutnjak, in front of guests, guests, guests from Bosnia and Herzegovina, Montenegro and Serbia. Beauty and joy pervade mother and son at this wedding in Belgrade.

Picture 13. Dance at the wedding

Branka and Željko, husband and wife with a long marriage experience, are calm — side by side, next to each other. Our dance is light. Hand in hand. My arm around her waist, hers over my shoulder. All around us, there is noisy rejoicing. Our peace and contentment are deep within us.

Picture 14. Montenegrin bouncing. The bride got married.

Completely uninvited, provoked by nothing from the outside, an unstoppable enthusiasm to dance, to jump Montenegrin at another wedding in Belgrade, on a boat on the Sava, near the confluence of the Danube, boiled out of me.

I look at this picture and rejoice. My heart and soul rejoice as I fly. I fly, fly, fly...

"My love, I don't know how long I've been standing here, I wish I could go back. You don't know that half of me stayed with you to follow you. My love, you are tired and without you I am making your bed on some fading start, I am looking for the light that I do not have."

Picture 15. Excursion to Vipazar

A beautiful day. Clear and sunny. Hand in hand, side by side. Smiles on our faces. Look straight at the one who is looking at us.

31

THE SON OF AN ADULT IS GETTING MARRIED

Picture 16. Ode to joy

That day has come. The first baby, the eldest son grew up and got married. The happy mother embraced both sons in a wide hug, with wide smiles, wide joy, and happiness in her chest.

It was the best wedding in Hotel "Podgorica".

"It will be easy for you without me
but how will I do without you
when hard days come
when all friends leave
when they smell of lilacs."

Picture 17. Ode to joy

Mother and daughter. Daughter and mother. The widest and tightest hug at the first wedding in the family.

UNTIL WE MEET AGAIN

The star has arrived. The time has come for him to get married too. A happy mother dances with her son at a wedding. Smiling, happy and joyful, she looks into his eyes. She gave birth to him and raised him to be able to create and support his family.

Picture 18. Dance for Zvjezdana for eternity

◊

This "Ode to Joy" could not last long. That beauty of our lives acts as an illusion, as a calm before the storm.

MORS IN TABULA

(Exitus letalis u 14:45h)

UNIVERSITY CLINICAL CENTER OF SERBIA
CLINIC FOR CARDIO SURGERY
INTENSIVE CARE DEPARTMENT
Treated since August 13, 2022. until 18.08.2022.

DISCHARGE LIST WITH EPICRISIS

Diagnosis: Stenosis valvulae mitralis non rheumatic

Signed by: Director of the clinic, Prof. Dr. Svetozar Putnik, cardiac surgeon; Head of the department, Ass. Dr. Ilija Bilbia, cardiac surgeon; Presiding physician, Ass. Dr. sci med Duško Terzić, a cardiac surgeon.

Seal: Republic of Serbia - Belgrade

Massive endocarditis of the mitral and aortic valves was diagnosed intraoperatively. The infectious process affected the entire subvalvular apparatus of MV. After the first attempt to separate the patient from the ECC, there is a drop in tension. The patient was returned to the mode of maximum work of ECC with the inclusion of maximum inotropic support. After prolonging the ECC, with maximum inotropic support, the patient was gradually weaned from the ECC. The competence of the replaced valves was verified by the TEE examination. Checked hemostasis. After the closure of the sternum, hemodynamic instability occurs again, the sternum was urgently opened, and heart massage was started. All applied resuscitation measures remain without an adequate response.

Mors in tabula (Exitus letalis at 14:45) is declared. A clinical autopsy is not required.

◊

The casket with the remains arrived at the chapel on Čepurci around nine o'clock in the evening. I hugged the dead coffin for a long time, sobbing bitterly and painfully.

Zvjezdan was next to the wall, turning around, spinning, fiddling, sobbing loudly and painfully

BELOVED BRANKA

I didn't know, I didn't believe, I didn't think that this was the end, that a disease had come that has no cure and that will take you away, however, too quickly. I believed and hoped that it would be different, even when I was listening to you, sitting across from you, how loudly and painfully you uttered the words: "Alone! I will do it myself!"

Where? Where are you going alone? On the road of no return. To death.

The thought that you will never again, after 42 years, enter our apartment, our house, your house, gives me stomach cramps and pain in my whole body.

Instead of arrivals and meetings, instead of everything, we got you, we have you packed in a coffin so that we never see, hear, or feel you alive again. Neither you nor us. You neither hear nor see.

There is only a picture of you with a wide smile, big teeth, and scattered hair for all those who knew you and for whom you were once a living being and a respected person, because of your deeds.

I wish you a better world and a better society than I was for you.
I am wailing and grieving!
I cry for you, my Branka.
I am crying out loud from severe, great pain!!!!
Today and forever!!!!!

Željko Vujović
Podgorica, 20.08.2022.

37

"Why are you gone, why are you gone,
When on young field flowers
Silent Midnight strings pearls together
A song flows through my chest
Why are you gone, why are you gone."

Picture 19. A wide smile, large chin, scattered hair

Picture 20. "To die is to not need another being."

For a long time, I read the document "Discharge list with epicrisis", analyzed it, studied it, and wanted to reject it as a confirmation, the lowest legal act. I wanted to find out that the cardiac surgeons from the University Cardiac Surgery Clinic in Belgrade were sloppy. Yes, they mechanically replaced heart valves like spark plugs on a car engine. That they didn't do everything necessary., instead of life, they sent me a death certificate.

I can't figure out how that happened. I refuse to accept that massive endocarditis of the mitral and aortic valves was diagnosed intraoperatively and that the infectious process affected the entire subvalvular apparatus of the MV.

I cannot understand and accept that the heart has completely disintegrated, that it cannot do what it exists for, that is, what it existed for.

I am silent. I stare blankly at the pictures on the wall of the living room, in the apartment, which she chose and placed to decorate the apartment.

"THE SOUL IS HEALED BY FORGETTING"

In my mind is the confirmation from the University Cardio-Surgical Clinic in Belgrade that she died. There. At their place. I don't know where that certificate is now. I put it away somewhere. It fools me. Again, the crazy idea that confirmation is the lowest legal act, that death requires a much higher legal act, is running through my mind.

Every time I enter the apartment, she seems to be there. In the living room, on the couch, he goes through the dining room, the corridor, and the room, to the balcony to spread the laundry. You can't see her, you can't hear her, but, so invisible and silent, she walks around the apartment.

In the cottage, on Durmitor, as well. The last time I was there, I didn't see her on the couch in the living room and I had a big crying fit.

From there, where she went, no one came back. I am not yet aware that she has left. I hold her, there, somewhere inside me, as if she is better there. I create an appearance, an illusion. I live in an illusion.

How can I forget her? It is easy for her now that she is in the Street of those whom no one disturbs.

I'm going out on the town. Clear autumn day. Everything is the same. Houses and unknown people pass through the streets of my city. Something tightens in my throat. I feel a pain in my chest.

THE WOMAN AND THE PSYCHIATRIST

People say that a professor's husband, who was a psychiatrist, died. After that, she went to his grave for a long time, threw stones at the grave, threw stones at the grave, and cursed loudly: Your mother's cunt! Why did you leave me?! Why?!!!

SADNESS

Grief is a reaction to the loss of something valuable, and important, to which an individual attaches special importance. A normal response to the loss of a loved object.

THE HERO OF OUR AGE [1]

"There are moments in life when your neighbor separates from you like a nail from the thumb on the right hand and leaves." You are then all reduced to one single gesture, one motive, and the same emotion, which is falsely displayed through thousands of intermediate feelings: you are reduced to that futile and profoundly unreasonable attempt to return him. What happens in such moments, on that day, maybe on a weekend, or in more invasive cases, in those months and years, is one of your strongest experiences in life. You are present in it as much as you could not be at your birth and how much you will not be at your death.

For the community, death is something ordinary every day. It's the same for you until your loved ones die. Moreover, the more unusual the death, the more sudden it is, the more the death is caused by an internal accident and not by external actions, and the more the community will instinctively distance itself from you. Formal expressions of condolence are used for this distance: when someone says you receive my condolences, they usually mean that the trouble will escape from me. That's what hospital forms are for, rules of behavior in the morgue, postmortem police reports... The system didn't let you down in your desperate attempts to get your loved one back, to get the nail on your right thumb back, but some living people avoided that. your destiny is reflected in them. In a way, it's a good thing that it is, because you will console yourself by telling yourself that they are to blame for the death of your loved one. What would you do without that comfort? How would you explain this loss to yourself?"

[1] Lermontov Mihail Jurjevič, *Hero of our time*, "Veselin Masleša", Sarajevo, 1974.

SEMIOTICS OF DARKNESS AND SEMANTICS OF SILENCE [2]

A man named Uve[3] was returning yesterday from Delta City, passed Velika Rijeka over the Crooked Bridge, continued along the street towards Zabjel, passed the football stadium, turned left onto the road leading to Ljubović, came to a metal gate with bars and entered the Street of those whom no one knows disturbing.

Clear, sunny, November day. Marble tombstones with gilded names. Again, he failed to simply find grave site number 262, plot 11, which he bought with his father's power of attorney and his father's money, in the summer of the penultimate year of the last, twentieth century. He was following path number 10. He did not see the fountain, which was his landmark to find the burial place he was looking for. Search. The fountain is on track number 11. It goes from track number 10 to track number 11, stepping on the green grass between the marble tombstones. See the fountain. He is directed towards her. Turning left, stepping on the green grass again, he comes to the marble tombstone at grave site number 262. Dark marble. Two pots with flowers. Around the grass. The letters of Branka's name still shine. Fathers and mothers have darkened. He puts his hand on the marble slab, looks up at the sky, and sighs deeply. It will stay a little longer. Fix the position of one flower pot. He stood up, sighed once more, several more times, and slowly headed towards the chapels and the exit towards Montenegrin Serdara Street. His gaze wanders in all directions. He will not stop at the names of people, who were once living beings, written on monuments. There is a large number of those he knew. He suppresses from his mind, from his memory, the names of those three evildoers from the time he

---

[2] Slavica Perović, *Life Lift*, New book, Podgorica 2012, p. 21 - 24
[3] Fredrik Bakman, *A man named Uve,* New book, Podgorica, 2018

worked at the Medical Institute. Their marble tombstones are in the same plot number 11, across the street from the fountain. Among the other tombstones, he can distinguish them located at the vertices of a large acute-angled triangle. Perhaps, a little, they stand out compared to the others, because their marble is darker. They are the source of darkness. "The impression is the experience of a lack of light. The day is clear, the sun is shining. The slope of the earth is almost unchanged on its path around the Sun. Where did that hint of darkness come from?"

[4]Exited through the gate closer to Ljubović, concerning the chapel, continued along the sidewalk of Montenegrin Serdara Street to the intersection with traffic lights near the "Sergije Stanić" Vocational School. Across the street from the school is now the "Union" hotel, built on the spot where the family house of his long-deceased neighbor Ilija Stanić used to be. He does not stop by the house that he inherited from his father and mother. The house is there, quite close, in the middle of a small, quiet, quiet street, hidden by newly built multi-story buildings. He crosses the intersection and continues straight, to the end of the Boulevard, to his apartment on the sixth floor. He has not yet accepted or understood that he will be alone in the apartment and that he is single. His children stopped being children a long time ago. They don't have, they don't express the need to contact him, call him, do something, or clean up something in the apartment, which, for many years, was also their apartment, their home. They have their apartments. They separated. He's thinking. He is always the one who answers them first. He keeps them there, somewhere in himself, in his throat, in his chest. He doesn't drop them. He cannot let them go, even though they have long since left, separated. Silence. A man named Uve is lying in bed. Wake up. He opens his eyes. It hasn't been distributed yet. He feels bad. His nose is blocked. Common cold. He will cancel his participation in today's hiking tour in the Kučki mountains, below Treskavac to Bukumir Lake. His gaze passes over the walls of the room, and the furniture. Everything is there, the same as it was when Branka

[4] Slavica Perović, *Life Lift*, New book, Podgorica, 2012, p. 25-26

left. Beds into the former matrimonial room, unmoved. On them are several plastic folders, left there temporarily, in an attempt to organize the chest of drawers by the window. Plastic bags filled with clothing intended for the Red Cross, leaning against the wall, are waiting. The wardrobe has not yet been sorted out.

What should he do?

Gets up. He makes tea. No one answers him. No one calls him. Will he call the children? To ask if he will come to visit them today.

He gave up.

ONCE YOU SHOULD LOOK AT YOURSELF IN THE MIRROR [5]

Look deeply into the mirror,
into the reflection of yourself.
That you look with your eyes open is not a lie,
it is not a poetic metaphor. That's you.
With the name your mother gave you, do you remember?
You, with the identity of success and defeat. Loss.
Unfulfilled and unfulfilled dreams
In search of peace with thoughts that swarm
like bees in hives in an apiary.
Do you see that face? Dark circles, gray hair?
A calm, wrinkled forehead between the eyes?
Unclear and indefinite chest tightness?
Tonight will be the New Year.
The first one, which she won't wait for.
People pass by on the street, through markets, cafes...
Emptiness in the chest. Emptiness and quiet sadness.
The great loneliness returns to consciousness.
A terrible feeling of helplessness.
She didn't bother anyone, and she had to go.
Forever,
Again should be taught.
To learn to enjoy oneself.
In himself and silence.
The relationship with the family should be nurtured.
The extended family is a resource.

---

[5] Pietra Fon Thielen, *Poetry and Prose,* "Female Mirror", Split, Dalmatia, Croatia, on 31.12.2022.

Family history,
contact with distant relatives
and remember that it is its own life
part of a larger story with many interesting characters.
Bert Hellinger is your father's age.
He was born the same year as your father.
He lived 21 years longer than him.
What is your family schedule like?

Picture 21. This is how the last year of the seventh decade of thetwentieth century greeted in the House of the JNA in Podgorica

A year and a half have passed since that summer of 1977. Look at this conceited but self-confident guy with his nose and chin up and this beautiful girl with a wide smile and blonde hair looking at him. It seems that she does not blame him for his conceit. Maybe he's not conceited, he's just happy and satisfied that this beautiful girl is next to him.

31.12.2023

This girl has it all. She radiates beauty and radiates joy to the environment, and to those who are around her.

Where did this bright figure go?

Picture 22. Branka at the dawn of New Year 1979

01.01.2023.

◊

I dreamed of her before dawn.

The kind with bangs

Like on a trip to Virpazar.

She was getting ready to go somewhere.

I asked her: Where are you going?

She didn't want to say.

I was spinning around her.

So tell me, at least, for God's sake!

She didn't tell me.

I woke up.

06.01.2023

Is this enough evidence for a person to come to terms with the fact that someone is no longer there? Many things are argued with someone over time, and what is a man?

And what will I do and how will I do it?
Little hands, little strength,
One straw among the whirlwinds... [6]

◊

"Well, my friend:

There comes a moment in life when you find out:
who is important to you, who was never important to you,
who will never be important to you again,
and who will always be important to you?

So don't worry about people from your past,
because there's a reason why they didn't
get involved in your present.

Happiness makes you better.
Temptation makes you stronger.
Grief makes you a man.
Failure makes you humble.
Only the strength of your personality
pushes you towards success and progress."

Glory and memory to my Branka!

Podgorica, February 18, 2023

---

[6] Petar II Petrović Njegoš, *The Mountain Wreath*, Obod, Cetinje, 1996.

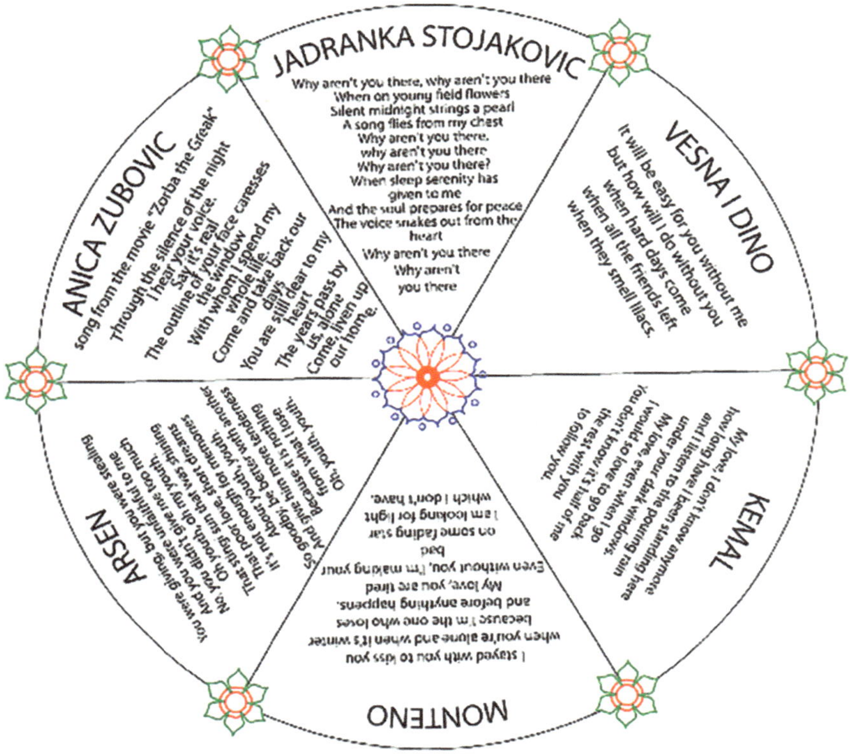

Zeljko Vujovic
December 12, 2022

There is no solution to destruction. Life is a carousel, it should be a game. What does the song "Birdhouse", sung by Gabi Novak, and what does the song "Game with no limits", performed by Toše Proeski, relate to?

GAME WITH NO LIMITS

If only I could wake up in the world of love without my old friends and these freaks who always followed me.
If only I could kiss you without bad memories of cold spring without the image of suffering that sticks with us.

Because my life is a game without limits, a tired story, tearing pages on which nothing is written.
Because my life is an eternal fall, when I add up the defeats, nothing remains, I'm still dragging my habits and that's all there is to it.

If only I could wake you up, make your coffee, bring you to
bed
to kiss you, but that doesn't exist.
If only I could fall in love with a little peasant girl in a
clearing
up in space so I can't see down.

Because my life is a game without limits, a tired story, a tearing of pages on which nothing is written.
Because my life is an eternal fall, when I add up the defeats, nothing remains, I'm still dragging my habits and that's all there is to it.

Sung by Toša Proeski

Author of music: Miroslav Rus **Author of lyrics**: Miroslav Rus **Author of arrangement:** Nikša Bratoš Video clip for the song "Game with no limits" from the promotion of the album "Game with no limits" Tvornica, Zagreb.
Source: https://www.youtube.com/watch?v=VMT50KhLlRw

A NOTE ABOUT THE AUTHOR

On the road less traveled

Željko Vujović was born on February 28, 1952 in Podgorica. He published the following books:

– Bosnia Needs To Be Passed - Aporias of Elijah of Thunder (2021)
– A small album of Memories - excerpts from the biography Torn from Oblivion (2020)
– From Nuclear Spin to Magnetic Resonance Imaging (2019)
– What language did my mother speak? (2018)
– Remembrance (2017)

He published scientific articles, of which the following stand out:

– Classification Model Evaluation Metrics (2021)
– Big Data and Machine Learning (2020)
– Magnetic Resonance Signal (2019)

He lives in Podgorica.

THE IMMORTAL SOUL

"If the East Sun gives birth to light,
if the being boils into bright rays
if the Earth is not an apparition,
the human soul is immortal."

THE SPACE IS SMALL, AND THE TIME IS GREAT

Alexa

www.ingramcontent.com/pod-product-compliance
Lightning Source LLC
Chambersburg PA
CBHW040848120626
46547CB00001B/81